IMPACT

IMPACT OF GLOBALIZATION ON INDIAN SOCIAL LIFE

DR ANSHUMALI PANDEY

Made with ♥ on the Notion Press Platform
www.notionpress.com

Contents

Prologue

Globalization has been defined as the process of rapid integration of countries and happening through greater foreign trade and foreign investment. In essence, it refers to increased possibilities for action between and among people in situations irrespective of geographical considerations as per the definition of social theorists. Due to economic liberalization and globalization, the world has become a "global village". There is increasing interaction among people of different countries. As a result food habits, dress habits, lifestyle and views are being internationalized. There has been both positive and negative impact of globalization on social and cultural values in India. There is no denying of the fact that globalization has brought cheers to people's life by opening new vistas of employment. It has also made inroads in the cultural heritage of this country.

Every step of movement towards economic, political and cultural modernization, taken by the state in India, is responded to by the people with an enhanced sense of self-consciousness and awareness of identity. Cultural modernization, sponsored by the forces of globalization, is resented if it encroaches upon or does not promote the core cultural values of society, its language, social practices and styles of life. The vigour of the renewed sense of self-awareness generated among the members of the local cultures and communities is such as to succeed in making adaptive reconciliation with the forces of globalization. The linkages both visible and invisible, defining the cultural interdependence among communities and regions in India which have existed historically, reinforce instead of threatening the national identity. These bonds seem to become stronger as India encounters the forces of modernization and globalization.

The term 'Globalization' is in itself self-explanatory. It is a global platform for maintaining evenness in the living mode of the individuals all over the world. Globalisation is the resultant of the interchange of worldly views, opinions and varied aspects of the culture all over the world. This is the method of giving the globalised world a way of intermixing of individuals from various segments, culture and lingos and figure out how to move and approach socially without harming and influencing every others' prestige and glory. Globalization highly affects social, fiscal, political, and mutual existence of nations. Plentiful hypothetical investigations exhibited that globalization mediates in a social existence of people that pertains various basic issues.

Globalization is depicted by scholars as the procedure through which social orders and economies are incorporated through cross-border flows of thoughts, correspondence, innovation, capital, individuals, finances, merchandise, administrations, services and information. The term globalization means international integration, the world trade prospects being opened, development of advanced means of communication, internationalization of financial markets, growing importance of MNC's and population migrations. It has also widened the scope of the mobility of persons, goods, capital, data and ideas. It is a way through which the dissimilar world is unified into one society.

The wave of globalization started entering and effecting India at the end of the last century and still the country is flowing with the present of global changes.

Globalization has both positive and negative effects all through the globe. May it be business, trade, and work exposure or the economic and financial status of the nation; no field is deserted from the scope of globalization. The culture and way of living of any nation does not just depict the region and dialect of the locale, yet it also shows with the attitude and mindset of its people. Indian culture is very rich for its legacy and assets, and the warm approach of its residents. India is bunch of flowers consisting of various religion, languages, food, cuisine and edibles, convention, custom, music, craftsmanship and architecture and so forth, packaged into a solitary unit of patriotism and solidarity.

The common factor of these varieties is the Indian attitude of greeting, welcoming, celebrating unitedly with immense friendship and harmony. This is the rich embodiment of the Indian culture that has pulled in numerous non-natives to remain back in India and blend into its interminable fragrance. When we analyze this rich culture with the globalization perspective, we can discover many inferences of westernization and blending of different attributes and societies into our delightfully woven cover. As every coin has two sides likewise globalization also has its positive and negative effects.

CHAPTER I

SOCIAL LIFE AND IMPORTANT SOCIAL INSTITUTIONS

Before going into the details of the Social life and Institutions it will be necessary to keep in mind that India is not a country of any monolithic tradition and there are a variety of religious, ethnic, regional cultural traditions which make this country a land of unity in diversity. Even the Hindus who form the majority of Indian population maintain a number of regional social and cultural patterns along with their languages. It reflects in their organizational hierarchies, practices of marriage, kinship system, status of woman etc. Similarly, each of the major religious communities has its social peculiarities and some variety of social practices. Yet, there is some common social approach of all the Indian communities with regard to their social behavior in public and their mutual interactions and inter-communal relations. It is the result of a continuous phenomenon of synthesis between different cultural communities over the centuries of co-existence and co-patriotic progress of the Indian people in the modern age. It is again a manifestation of the attitudes and outlook of the people of this land towards oneself and others including non-human animal world and the nature as a whole which we specifically call Indian.

There are a number of social practices and rituals which the people of this land seem to observe individually or privately implying their concern for the whole humanity and the nature termed as 'jeeva' and 'jagat'. Many of these rites also imply social interactions with persons of different strata and communities. Some of the sacraments are observed exclusively to maintain particular family and cultural tradition. On the other hand, you can see the inter-communal greetings and meetings at the time of religious festivals of one-another community. There are a number of occasions when people use to assemble and interact. These may be of both secular and religious nature. While the religious assemblages are mostly the part of the age-old religio-cultural traditions of India, so many old and new outlets of social gatherings have developed over the ages like musical concerts, theatres, cinemas, sports'-events etc. which speak for the social life of the peoples in this land.

As far as the social institutions are concerned we will have to look into it as per each major religious community which has its own system of social classes and hierarchy, marriage and family customs, kinship bonds etc. The Hindus in particular have a complex social structure based on caste-system and in spite of the modern secular ethos the inter-caste and intra-caste relations become a curious subject of observation. The practice of marriage within one's own caste is a corollary to the caste system of the Hindus. There are a variety of other regional and tribal social institutions also which have to be taken into account for their peculiar systems and practices.

CHAPTER II

INDIAN SOCIAL LIFE

We shall try to know about the social life of the people at two levels. Firstly, it is such practices and rituals of social value which are performed by individuals individually or privately. Secondly, it is those areas of social interaction which demand social appearance and social courtesies.

Individual Social Practices:

As we know India is a land of different cultural and religious communities whose social behaviour is mainly embedded in their religious practices. The major cultural tradition in India belongs to the Hindus who have evolved or adopted a number of practices over the years in their daily life which are a part of their religion or religious activities. At the same time, they reflect their relationship with the humanity and the nature or environment. The first and the foremost is the concept of three debts, every man is supposed to be born with-'Rishi rina' (debt to the Sage/teacher), 'Pitri rina' (debt to the Parents/Ancestors) and 'Deva rina' (debt to the gods). He is obliged to repay it through the practice of 'trivargas', i.e. 'dharma' (rightful conduct as prescribed by sages and scriptures), 'artha' (adoption of rightful means of livelihood) and 'kama' (aesthetics and rightful way to progeny) which leads him to 'moksha' (the final salvation). All these four are called the four 'Purusharthas' and all these 'Purusharthas' are expected to be observed through the four successive 'Ashramas' (Orders/Scheme of life)-the 'Brahmacharya' (the period of learning the sacred scriptures under a teacher), the 'Garhastha' (the period of householder-ship), the 'Vanaprastha' (the period of renunciation) and the 'Sanyasa' (the final stage of solitary religious life). However, the focus is more upon the life of the householder who is supposed to undertake a host of responsibilities and perform a number of duties as his daily rites and other commitments to his family and the society.

He is expected to perform the 'Pancha Mahavratas' (the five great rites) as his daily routine. Beginning with 'Brahma yajna' (daily offerings to the brahmanas or sages) a householder is obliged to perform 'Pitri yajna' (daily oblations to ancestors), 'Deva yajna' (daily oblations to gods), 'Bhuta yajna' (daily oblations to evil spirits) and 'Nri' or 'Manushya yajna' (offering hospitality to guests).

Besides the above mentioned duties the Hindu way of life is bound with a number of 'Samskaras' (Sacraments) right from the conceiving of the child in the womb of its mother to the death of a person. The Samskaras vary in number in different scriptures, viz. 11 in Grihya Sutras, 40 in the Gautam Dharma Sutra, 18 in Vaikhanas Dharmasutra, 16 in Smriti Chandrika and 13 in some other Dharmashastras. Important among these may be enumerated as 'Garbhadhan' (lawful intercourse with the wife with the intention of progeny), 'Punsavan' (a rite for getting strong male child), 'Seemantonnayan' (a rite to protect the child when it is still in the womb of the mother), 'Jatakarma' (a rite at the birth of the child), 'Namakarana' (Naming of the child), 'Nishkramana' (taking the child out of the house for the first time), 'Annaprashana' (feeding the child with food for the first time), 'Choorakarana' or 'Chaula' (shaving of the head of the child for the first time), 'Karnabhedan' (piercing of ears to enable the child to wear earrings or ornaments), 'Vidyarambha' (a rite of bathing for the commencement of education first at home), 'Upanayan' (the initiation of scriptural education under a 'guru' or teacher normally at some 'gurukula' or teacher's house called 'ashrama') to be followed by 'Vedarambha' and 'Godana' and finally 'Samavartana' (convocation address by the teacher on the completion of education). The 'Vivaha' (marriage) and the 'Antyeshti' (the funeral rites) are next two Samskaras which complete the life-cycle of a Hindu. Although all the above mentioned Samskaras and whatever else are prescribed in between them in other scriptures are to be observed privately but most of them are performed in the presence of the kith-n-kin as well as such persons of the community/society like the barber, servants and the presiding priest or the teacher who are required for the performance of the rites. Most of the time they are accompanied or followed by community feasts also.

Another very important feature of the social obligations of a Hindu householder is offering hospitality to the visitor. In Indian ethos a guest is treated as a god, 'atithi devo bhava'. It corresponds to the 'manushya yajna' among the five great rites enumerated above. Then offering alms to the brahmanas, recluses or the 'sanyasis' is also considered a pious duty and as regular rite. Further, a householder is never expected to refuse alms to any beggar or destitute approaching him. Offering gifts to friends and family relations and organizing charities within one's means are some other dimensions of the social obligation of an individual and family.

The Hindu view of life is closely associated with the nature and environment. Hindus consider the rivers as their source of life and call them mother. Worshipping everything living or non-living, trees/vegetation, rivers, ponds and mountains and relating a number of birds, animals and even fish to certain godly entities or gods/ goddesses speaks volume about this trait of Hindus. This is further extended to the ethos of non-violence and vegetarianism in a large Hindu community. Then the ethics of personal and social hygiene should also be not taken sight of. Thus, a Hindu is always supposed to be concerned with his personal conduct and social obligations both overtly or covertly.

However, a tourist or a stranger should not be made to confuse that all these ideals and ethics are thoroughly observed or practiced by all the Hindus of present day Indian society.

A lot of elasticity and flexibility in actual practices is also granted and so many relaxations are recommended in the scriptures itself that there is sufficient scope of deviating from an ideal position. One may undoubtedly find some adherents of the dictates in the strictly traditional families, in smaller cities and countryside, isolated pockets in hilly or remote areas and particularly in the regions of southern India, but this too is mainly confined to the brahmana community, and even very few among them might be practicing it with the true spirit of the religion and in the real sense of the words. Otherwise it ought to display their pride and vanity and becomes a subject of hypocrisy. Because a larger majority of the Hindus was not enlisted in the above mentioned scheme of life and with the adoption of new education system and new modes of livelihood and the new system of economy, technology etc., the basics of the social obligations are often been ignored and very little concern is visible for keeping the things in order.

As far as the Buddhist and Jain traditions are concerned, there we may find some definite social ethics which an individual is supposed to follow. The observance of the principles of self-restrain and non-violence are the two essential features of most of these communities even today. The adherents of Sikh faith are more known for their service, 'kar seva' to others in their personal capacity.

The Muslims in India alike the followers of Islam everywhere as individuals are expected to observe purity, 'waju', and truthfulness and offer charities, 'jaquat', to the needy peoples as per scriptural rules. And so is the Christian community in India which is supposed to be bound by the ten-commandments in order to maintain personal morality and serving the humanity. But it should also be kept in mind that both the Christianity and Islam are the religions mainly based on community behaviour and apart from general human and moral ethics they do not prescribe any specific rites or rituals to be observed by individuals privately with whatever personal and social motives. The general rule of the gap/difference between the scriptural/religious prescriptions and the actual practices, however, apply to most of the peoples irrespective of the faith they claim to be following.

General Social Practices:

Apart from the obligations which the people carry individually, various communities in India have other traditional social duties to fulfill. The caste-system in the Hindus, which we will discuss in detail later in this unit, made it obligatory upon the people to serve or help one-another as per the duties prescribed for their caste. Traditionally, this was also bound in the 'jajmani-system' which was, in a way, a system of local rural interdependence of different communities and the rural lords. This meant the service to the rural lord, the jajman, by different occupational peoples like iron-smith, goldsmith, carpenter, washer, barber, bamboo-worker, scavenger, labourers and all who fell in the category of 'kamin', 'pardhan', 'purjan' or 'parjan' or 'parjania' in the sense of the subject people. This they performed only in lieu of the protection and reward and occasional gifts normally in kind, such as grain, fodder, clothing etc. Though the term originally referred to the client for whom a brahmana priest performed rituals, but later on it came to be referred to the patron or recipient of specialized services. This system of jajmani might also occur between other land holders, farmers and other village professional/skilled craftsman/artisans and non-skilled workers in the same fashion. And, quite interestingly, this system worked among all types of rural folk and their masters or lords irrespective of the religious identities of the people. The jajmani system remained the part of the 'jamindari' system which was implemented in colonial India as a system of permanent settlement for the collection of revenue. However, the system of jajmani as well as jamindari was abolished with coming of the present republic of India, but some rudiments of the system may still be found in the rural areas, particularly the remote ones. The 'gram-sabha' and 'panchayata', the village assembly and council respectively, served multifold purpose of social, administrative and judicial life of the village community in India.

A very common feature of the social practice of the Hindus can be deduced from the age-old tradition of pilgrimage and gatherings for bathing and worshipping at some holy place and established or popular temples. This also includes visits to places and 'dargahs' or tombs of Sufi saints and many other saints of repute.

Since India is a multi-cultural land various classes and communities have learnt to co-exist in harmony and brotherhood. There are numerous occasions of showing social courtesies to the one another. While the Hindu expression of welcoming a person is 'Namaste' or 'Pranam', the Muslims say 'Adab Arz', 'Salam' or 'Salam vale kum' to be responded by 'Vale kum salam', the Sikh say 'Sat Shri Akal' and the Christians say 'Hello', and so are some other ways of salutations of different regional and smaller communities. Almost all the communities invite and welcome persons of different communities also besides their own kith-n-kin at different family functions like marriage etc. They are also in the habit of throwing party or feasts to their friends and neighbourhood at some celebrations. Inter-communal interactions are quite visible with greetings and meetings at the occasions of Diwali, Holi, Id-ul-Fitr, Id-ul-juha, Christmas, Ishtar, Guru Nanak Jayanti, Lohiri in Pujab, Pongal in South India, Ganesha puja in Maharashtra, Navaroj etc. Then there are occasions of general public interests like independent day, republic day, ..

Different communities as well as individuals and social organizations have a traditional way organizing charities like offering of food and clothing to the poor at religious occasions and otherwise. Erection or construction of 'dharmashalas', 'yatri-shalas' or 'sarais' or rest-houses for the pilgrims, temples etc. have been a common practice of the rich or elite class of the society in India. The Sikkha community is particularly known for organizing daily and special langars at Gurudwaras and elsewhere, and doing 'kar-seva'.

CHAPTER III

INDIAN SOCIAL INSTITUTIONS

Each and every major religious communities of India have their own social institutions like social classification, marriage prerequisites and conditions, family customs and kinship bonds as per their religious dictates. Since the Hindu communities are the oldest and predominant communities in India, the system of castes and some social taboos prevalent among them has infiltrated into or influenced all the other communities of India in one form and way or other. Among several factors for this feature of Indian society, one major reason seem to be the emergence or formation of a majority of all other major religious communities in India from within the social segments of Hindus during different historical eras.

Hindus:

Castes: Traditionally the Hindu society is a caste based society and the castes are established as institutions in their own right. Theoretically it is the four classes of the people called 'chaturvarnas' put in a hierarchical order such as brahmanas, kshatriyas, vaishyas and shudras respectively which form the social organization of the Hindus inherited from the grand old Vedic times. This is supposed to have meant a classification of people based on a broad division of labour such as the brahmanas as priests and teachers, Kshatriyas as rulers and warriors, vaishyas as producers and traders and the shudras just as manual labourers or servants. But for all the practical reasons this classification did not remain confined to just the form of labour or occupation a person or a community was associated with, instead a person became to be identified by its birth in on one or other community known as caste.

Further the qualities and attributes associated with certain occupations were also assumed to be the permanent part of the personality of a person with which his family or caste is identified. One noticeable element in this system of varnas and castes is that while the varnas are just four, the castes are innumerable which owe their origin to multiple factors like heredity or lineage, occupation, technique of occupation, skill, political status, historical and geographical connections, religious and cultural peculiarities, social acceptance or rejection in the mainstream culture, and many others. However, all these castes are finally assumed to the part of the fourfold division of the society known as varnas and each one of these is bracketed with one or other varna or have found position in between latter as mixed castes. Their social status is also defined accordingly which may, however, vary region to region as per its historical, political, economic and cultural background with regard to brahmanas, of course, who for being considered as the custodians and supervisors of this system have to remain always on top of the social hierarchy.

A caste is different from a tribe in the sense that a tribe is a wholesome compact of the people having no social stratification or hierarchy within or with regard to other communities, whereas a caste is weighed against other castes in a broader and complex social system. Castes are often divided in sub-castes. Since a majority of castes happened to be socially bracketed with the shudras as lower or lowest communities as untouchables or even as segregated and isolated tribes, the constitution of modern republic of India has made provisions for their empowerment through special attention and affirmative action programme by earmarking them as Scheduled castes and Scheduled tribes and other backward castes (OBC).

There have been two outstanding features of the Hindu caste system. One is the marriage in one's own community/ caste and the other is the restriction of dining with anybody, particularly with the persons of lower castes.

Hindu Marriage: One of the most important attractions in India for a tourist from abroad is witnessing the marriage ceremonies of the Hindus in particular. Marriage in the Hindus is an essential sacrament which is not merely solemnized for the sake of pleasure in the form of a contract. Rather, it is a religious duty with the objective of repaying one's debt to his ancestors by advancing his generations. The precondition in a Hindu marriage is the selection of both the girl and the boy from the same caste with the objective of maintaining the purity of blood or birth which may be considered a type of endogamy. On the other, there are certain restrictions within one's own caste which may be termed as exogamy. The exogamy was subjected to the marriage between one's own 'gotra' and 'sapinda'. The 'gotra' lineage means descent from a common mythical ancestor or a 'rishi' (sage). Originally, it is considered, the 'gotras' were only eight but gradually there number rose to thousands. The 'gotra' exogamy, however, no more is a valid restriction and the people are also not giving much importance to it. The 'sapinda' restriction means avoiding marriage between persons related by blood up till five generations on the mother's side and seven to the father's side.

Though the breach to this is not penalized but it remains one of the considerations for the settlement of marriage. It appears that the marriage between cousins were earlier permissible but later came to be discredited. In some communities in south and south-west and western part of India we still find practice of marriage between cousins or 'sapindas' of the second-third order. For example, marriage with 'mama's' (maternal uncle's) daughter is a priority in some communities.

There has always been a possibility of inter-caste marriage. Theoretically it could take place between the male of a higher caste and female of a lower caste, at least the immediate lower caste. This form of inter-caste marriage is called 'anuloma' or right order of marriage. But marriage in the inverse order of caste was not appreciated and particularly any connubian with the lowest caste was not approved. All such restrictions have gone by the adoption of the democracy in independent India.

Similarly, polygamy (having more than one wife at a time) was acceptable to Indian society earlier, though it was mainly the privilege of elite. There were practices of polyandry (having more than one husband at a time) also in some hill tribes of India which is still allowed as some specific regional tribal customs. But both polygamy and polyandry is now prohibited for the mainland culture of Hindus.

There are eight types of marriages identified by the Hindu law givers. These are –brahma, daiva, arsha, prajapatya, gandharva, asura, rakshasa and paishacha. In brahma form, the marriage is settled by the parents and the marriage is solemnized in the presence of a brahmana priest. The bride's father hands over his daughter to the groom with some dowry of ornaments and clothes. In the daiva form the daughter is offered to any officiating priest at the end of a 'srauta' sacrifice. A cow and an ox or a pair of oxen is offered by the bridegroom to the bride's father instead, as a matter of courtesy in the arsha form of marriage. The Prajapatya is similar to brahma form. The only difference is that the joint performance of certain rituals by the husband and the wife at the time of wedding and thereafter is envisaged in this type of marriage. This, perhaps, refers to the performance of 'saptapadi', i.e. giving mutual assurance of commitments to one-another by the bride and the bridegroom. The 'gandharva' form of marriage is in fact a union of love, a marriage between two youths with personal desire in which no consent of the parents/guardians of both the parties have been sought for. In the 'asura' form a formal sale of the daughter by her father to the groom takes place. The price is settled as a pair of oxen or anything. The 'rakshasa' form means marrying a girl after her forceful abduction against the consent of the bride's family. And, the 'paishacha' implies marrying a girl while she is unconscious or out of her senses without the consent of any responsible persons. Among these eight forms of marriage the first four are said to be lawful which entails the consent of the concerned parties or at least the father of the bride. Among these four neither the 'daiva' nor 'arsha' forms are now in practice. The form of marriage which is most popular in the present day Hindu society is a sort of mixture of 'brahma' and 'prajapatya'. Whereas the last four are arbitrary and the last two are abhorrent. While the 'gandharva' form of marriage could never be right off in any age and situation, the last three are now not valid in the eyes of law.

In the earlier days it is known that it was the groom's party which had to seek and select a bride or match for the former. But the custom has almost reversed in later and present times. Ones the match making is over the ceremonies of betrothal and engagements commence. The boy's mother consents to the choice of the bride by doing the rite of 'god-bharai' or 'roka' and a similar act is done on the part of the girl's family called 'var-ichchha' or 'barikchchha' or 'chhekaiya' in the vernacular languages which may even be in the form of the ceremony of 'tilak' more popular in the eastern part of India. Different other customs in this regard are also prevalent in other regions of India. It is now being replaced by a common ceremony of engagement in urban societies in big cities. Then it is the practice of bridegroom's party called 'barat', composed of male (now also female in urban areas) kith-n-kin along with family friends, to reach and received and welcomed with a feast at the girl's house or the venue of marriage as per earlier agreement for actual marriage. The rites of actual marriage take place thereafter during auspicious period pre-decided and presided over by the family priests. This includes chanting of 'mantras' in order to propitiate the deities and the performance of 'saptapadi' around the holy fire. Finally, the groom's party departs along with the bride and the latter is in turn received and welcomed at the groom's house.

There was also the practice of child marriage since it devolved upon the father of a girl to get his daughter married to a suitable match within three months as soon as the girl reached her age of puberty or even before that. Otherwise, he was considered to be accumulating sin with the passing of each and every period of menstruation of his daughter. But now such a practice has been prohibited by law. Similarly, the possibilities of divorce on the part of both the man and woman and remarriage of woman and the widow, although enunciated in early Hindu scriptures, had come to a stop in the traditional Hindu society have reappeared in the modern times. Several legislations have been drawn to check the wrongful traditions of marriage with amendments in Hindu Marriage Act. With the 'The Hindu Widows Remarriage Act', 1856; 'The Child Marriage Act', 1929; 'The Hindu Marriage Disabilities Removal Act', 1946; 'The Hindu Marriage Validity Act', 1949; 'The Hindu Marriage Act', 1955; 'The Special Marriage Act', 1954 and 'The Dowry Prohibition Act', 1961 so many insensitive and irrational traditional practices have now been restricted or removed.

Hindu Family and Kinship: Our purpose here is to know about the structure and form of Hindu family and guiding spirit behind the functioning of this institution without going into a deeper conceptual and sociological debate over the subject. The Hindu family was undoubtedly patriarchal. As the order of the householder, a married man, remained the nucleus of all the social and religious activities the system of the family has a major role to play in it. While a number of rites or sacraments an individual could observe individually, there were a number of other duties and responsibilities which could be shared with other family members and which could be smoothly observed in a larger or joint family system. The families tied with agricultural land in the rural set up and those operating trade at bigger scale in the cities ought to have a joint family system with the elder of the house as its chief. A family could remain un-split until third and fourth generation, i.e. starting from father as the head of the family to his sons, grandsons and great grandsons or as a householder having his old/retired parents, his sons and grandsons all living together. But, individual units having just a householder, his wife and their children who have not grown enough to have separate dwellings were also not unknown, particularly in the poorer class. According to K. M. Kapadia (Marriage and Family in India, Bombay, 1966, p. 220) early family in India was not joint or patriarchal alone. Side by side with the patriarchal families, we had individual families too.

A Hindu householder is expected to maintain the holy fire which is required for the performance of most of the daily rites. He is liable for the maintenance of his wife and children and also for the education and marriage of his sons and daughters. One of the most essential duties of a householder is offering 'tarpan' to his ancestors. The funeral rite or 'antyeshti' and 'sraddha' are two important features of the life of a householder. It is with this objective we notice a number of Hindus visiting Prayag, Kashi and Gaya as a matter of final 'pinda dana' (offering to ancestors once for all).

Kinship: It is a social relationship based upon family relatedness. A kin group may be explained as a group united by ties of blood or marriage. The circle of kinship originates from the paternal and maternal relations. Beyond the primary relationship or primary kin like father, mother, sister, brother, husband, wife, son and daughter, each of them may have his or her own circle of primary kin who would a secondary and tertiary kin to oneself. If a father's brother is a first kin to the father, he is a secondary kin to his son. Similarly, if a father's sister is a first kin to the father, she is secondary kin to his son. Furthermore, if a son of the brother of your father is first kin to his own father and secondary kin to your father, he is a tertiary kin to you. Likewise, the circle of primary kinship expands to secondary and tertiary kinship and so on. In a Hindu family this kinship is quite prized and more than a formal relationship.

'Baba' or 'dada-dadi' (paternal grandparents), 'nana-nani' (maternal grandparents) or on the reverse 'pota-poti' (son's son and daughter) and 'nati-natini' (daughter's son and daughter) are secondary kin in the order, but they may be more dearer/affectionate emotionally as well as for all the practical purpose. Similarly, a 'chacha' or 'kaka' (brother of the father) and a 'bua' or 'phua' (sister of the father) are considered to be a very close kin who may even have direct or indirect control over the family affairs if the situation so arises. Similarly, 'mama' (mother's brother) and 'mausi' (mother's sister) are also considered very close kin, and in some regions like Maharashtra and also in South 'mama' has some special status among all other kin. Then chacha's wife 'chachi', 'mama's wife 'mami', bua's husband 'phupha' and mausi's husband 'mausa' are also among the list of close kin. 'Bhabhi', the wife of the brother and 'jija' the husband of the sister are some most important members of the family.

In India people very much cherish the relations between the first cousins on both the sides, like chachera bhai, chacheri bahan, mamera bhai, mameri bahan, phuphera bhai, phupheri bahan, mausera bhai and mauseri bahan. As has been told earlier the closeness of relations may go even beyond this circle. The kids of the brothers and sisters and the first cousins also have their share in this relationship circuit. While there is a general custom of exchange of gifts among the kin group, one very important feature of this bond is perceptible is the need and presence of these one or other kin, mama-mami, bua-phupha, bhai-bhabhi in particular, for performing certain ceremonial rites at the time of marriage and the like occasions. This is the way how a Hindu family engages and involves its kinsfolk in various family ceremonies.

The rural India has another noticeable feature of relationship called pattidari or patidari. The family group having parted with other family members in terms of landed property is called pattidar or patidar. The relations with them may or may not be in harmony, however, it is tried to put a healthy face at least at the ceremonial occasions of either group for the sake of the society. The social ties in the rural India are further reflected in considering the daughter of any family of a village as a daughter of the whole village, at least at the emotional level, when married to a person of another place.

Muslims:

Broadly speaking, Muslims are divided into two divisions: Shias and Sunnis. It has nothing to do with the racial or occupational factors as found in the origin of various castes in Hindu society. The two groups follow different norms and social practices in certain areas, but generally it is the Sunni Law that has prevailed in India because the Shias are in lesser number in this country. Muslims are also divided into three other groups called Ashraf, Azlab and Arzal. The Saiyeds (tracing their origin from the Prophet Muhammad's daughter Fatima), Sheikhs, Pathans and a few others belong to the Ashraf. Most of the artisans and craftsmen like Momins (weavers), Mansooris (cotton cleaners), Ibrahims (barbeer) etc. belong to the Azlab and Halalkhor and the like belong to the Arzal group. The Ashrafs are the noble-born, the Azlabs are low-born, and the Arzals are the lowest of all. The Arzals may also be taken as untouchables among the Muslims, as they were not even allowed to enter the Mosque even, nor they were permitted to use public graveyards. This division, however, is purely based on the socio-economic basis and not on religion. The Shias and Sunnis on the one hand and the Ashrafs, the Azlabs and the Arzals on the other hand are endogamous groups. Intermarriage between them is not prohibited but is not appreciated.

Marriage in Muslim Community: In the Muslims the marriage is called 'nikah' which is a sort of civil contract between the bride and bridegroom in the presence of witnesses. It should not be taken merely as a contract for legal sexual relationship and procreation of children. It is also a religious duty, devotion and an act of 'ibadat'. One can reach 'jannat' or fall in 'dojakh' on the compliance and non-compliance of this duty respectively. It is called 'sunnat muwakkidal'. However, it is not laid down as a sacrament in the Muslims as it is there with the Hindus.

In the Muslims it is on the part of the boy's family to approach the family of the girl to find a match for him. There is no ceremony like betrothal before going for actual rituals of marriage in the Muslims. Rather the whole ceremony of 'nikah' includes both the proposal and acceptance at the same time. The bridegroom makes a proposal to the bride just before the wedding ceremony in the presence of two witnesses and a Maulavi (priest). It is necessary that both the proposal and its acceptance must be at the same meeting. A proposal made at one meeting and its acceptance at another meeting does not constitute a 'regular marriage' (sahi nikah), though it is not considered as 'invalid marriage' (batil). It is considered simply as an 'irregular marriage' (fasid). Further, female testimony has altogether been rejected in Muslim marriage; so the proposal and the acceptance of marriage contract must be witnessed by two male Muslims. One male and two females will not do.

The fasid or controversial marriages are: absence of witnesses at the time of making or accepting the proposal, fifth marriage of a man (because four wives are permissible, though not always appreciated without genuine reasons), marriage in a period when a woman is undergoing iddat (period of seclusion for three menstrual periods for a woman after the death of or divorce by her husband to ascertain whether she was pregnant), and deference of religion between husband and wife. The marriage of a man with a kitabia (Jew or Christian meaning those who follow the holly books) is sahi marriage but with one who worships either idol or fire is fasid marriage. However, a man can marry a non Muslim girl if he believes that her idolatry is nearly nominal but a Muslim woman under no circumstances is permitted to marry even with a kitabia. There are restrictions regarding polyandry and marriage with some consanguineous kin (e.g. mother, mother's mother, sister, sister's daughter, mother's sister, khala (mausi), father's sister phuphi (bua), daughter's daughter) or with an affinal kin (wife's mother, wife's daughter, son's wife). Yet another example of batil marriage is the marriage of a person with two such women who are related with each other in such a way that had any of these two women been a man cannot marry his sister-in-law (wife's sister) during his wife's lifetime. Batil marriage does not create any rights or obligations between the two parties. The children in such marriages are also considered illegitimate. It is only the valid or sahi marriage that confers upon wife the right of dower, maintenance and residence in the husband's house. Fasid or irregular marriage can be terminated by either party either before or after consummation by saying "I relinquish thee". If, however, consummation has taken place, children will be legitimate and will be entitled to inherit property. Similarly, wife also becomes entitled to dower.

Since marriages in Muslims are in the nature of a contract, it is expected that only the adults and sane people are allowed to undergo this rite. Child marriage and marriage of the people of unsound mind is not recognized. According to Muslim Personal Law, the child marriage can take place in the presence and with the consent of rightful guardians of the child, a boy or a girl. Firstly it is paternal line of the close kin and in the absence of it the close maternal line is permitted to sign the contract. Such a marriage can be revoked in the case of fraudulence or negligence on the part of the guardians involved. There are different specific conditions for such nullification in regard to a boy child and a girl child.

The third essential of the Muslim marriage is that the doctrine of equality must be observed. Though there is no legal prohibition to contract marriage with a person of low status, yet such marriages are looked down upon. Similarly, though run-away marriages (called kifa) are not recognized, yet girls do run away and marry with boys of their choice irrespective of whether they enjoy high or low status. Among the Sunnis social inferiority on the part of bridegroom could a ground for cancellation of marriage but not among the Shias. The fourth essential of the Muslim marriage happened to be the preference system in mate selection. The first preference was to be given to parallel cousin and then to cross-cousins. However, though both forms of parallel cousin marriage (chachera and mausera) were practiced in cross-cousins, phuphera type was not sanctioned. But, presently such practice of cousin-marriages is not much preferred.

Dower or Mahr: Dower is a sum of money or other property which a wife is entitled to get from her husband in consideration of the marriage. Under the Muslim Law, dower is an obligation imposed upon husband as a mark of respect to wife; it is thus not bride-price. Amount of dower may be fixed between two parties (called specified), and minimum specified amount cannot be less than ten dirhams, but for the maximum, there is no limit. When the amount is not specified, but is given whatever is considered to be proper, it is called proper dower (mutat). Amount of the dower cannot be reduced by the groom side and can be fixed either before or after or at the time of the marriage.The dower which is payable on demand is called 'prompt' dower and one which is payable on the dissolution of marriage, that is, after husband's death or divorce, is called 'differed' dower. Among the Shias, where there is no stipulation, the dower is presumed to be prompt, but among the Sunnis, it cannot be so presumed. Dower is also associated with the consummation of marriage. In case, the separation is due to wife's own initiatives, she is not entitled to any dower, if there is no consummation of the marriage. Under the Muslim Law, a widow can retain her husband's property (estate) till her dower is paid. She has the same claim in his property as other creditors have. A woman's right to dower is, however, extinguished if the divorce is either khula or mubarat, because in both the systems, the spouses mutually agree to dissolve their marriage.

Muta: It is a temporary form of marriage settled by a man and a woman with their mutual consent and without the intervention of the kin. This type of marriage a Muslim man can practice with even non-Muslim Jew and Christian girl but, a woman cannot contract such marriage with a non-Muslim. This type of marriage, however, is not popular in India and Pakistan either, perhaps due to insecurity of wife's right and children.

Divorce: Under the Muslim Law the contract of marriage can be dissolved either with the intervention of the court or without its intervention.

A Muslim marriage can be broken either by husband at his will (called talaq) or by the mutual consent of husband and wife called 'Khula' or 'kohl' and 'mubarat'. Talaq may or may not be revocable and irrevocable. Talaq may be given in any one of the following three ways: (a) Talaq-e-Ahasan, (b) Talaq-e-Hasan and (c) Talaq-e-ul-Bidat. Talaq-e-Ahasan is considered to be more approved form of divorce. In addition to these three types of talaq, Shariat Act of 1937 makes a mention of three other kinds of divorce too-(i) Illa, (ii) Zihar and (iii) Lian. The observation of iddat is an important consideration in the matter of divorce.

The family bonds and the kinship in the Muslims in India are not much different from the Hindus apart from the liberties in the 'sapinda' considerations in the matter of marriages.

Sikhs:

Sikhism began with the preaching of Guru Nanak Dev which its philosophy to different spiritual sources of Hindus and Muslims. It believed in 'nirguna' form of God and bestowed its faith in Guru Grantha Saheb, i.e. the collection of teachings and prayers of its Gurus. Sikhism has a tradition of ten Gurus and the last among them Guru Govund Singh prescribed the five signs for all the Sikhs which are the present identity of all the Sikhs. These are the five 'Ks': kesha (long hair and beard), kangha (comb), kara (bangle), kripan (dagger) and kachchha (shorts/ underwear). He also founded the 'Khalsa' means pure who were supposed to dedicate their whole life to protect and promote Sikhism.

Society: Sikhism is a religion based on the equality of men in the eyes of God as well as among themselves. Since a number of 'pantha' (sub-sects) within Sikhism have emerged over the centuries of its growth, there are some specific rituals and customs practiced by each of them. This reflects in their attire, turban and other symbols. The Nihangas, Nirankaris, Dera Sachcha Baba, Raidasis and like panthas are its example.

It is important to notice that since the majority of Sikh community has formed from erstwhile Hindu communities, the latter sometimes reflect their earlier social positions in spite of joining Sikhism. Though there is no practice of endogamy in such social classes of Sikhs in actual sense of the word, but for all practical purposes they prefer to interact and marry within the people of their own social class. However, this has nothing to do with the social philosophy of Sikhism as religion and all such features are mainly the reflection of the socio-economic background of different Sikh communities.

Marriage: Marriage is regarded a pious sentiment in Sikhism. It is a bond of life and thereafter. Nevertheless, the marriage rites in Sikhism are very short and easy which may be described as follows:

It is for parents to decide the relation of bride and bridegroom first. Then on a pious day father of the bridegroom takes the party to the bride's house or the venue already fixed or to some Gurudwara. Marriage party is received and a dinner/luncheon is arranged in its honour. Next or the same day, as per the situation demands, Granth Sahib is recited and it is around this the marriage is performed. The bride and the bridegroom jointly circumbulate the Granth Sahib four times. The bridegroom leads with a sword (in case) in his hand in this act. The Sikh family and kinship is organized almost in the fashion of Hindus. A family compact is very much visible in a Sikh family, whereas the individuality of a person is also respected.

Christians:

We find social stratification among Christians of India too. Firstly, it is the old division of the Protestants and Catholics which prevails in India also. The Catholics are further sub-divided as Latin Catholics and Syrian Catholics. Each group and sub-group is an endogamous group. Catholics do not marry with Protestants and Latin Catholics do not marry with Syrian Catholics. Apart from this sectarian division Christians in India do also reflect their social biases and taboos in keeping social relations with one or other Christian community with regard to their social position and historical background. There are elite and lower groups in Christians as well irrespective of the philosophy of brotherhood in Christianity.

Philosophically the objective of marriage in the Christian society is same as in the other major communities. Here of course religion has great significance this institution is suppose to have a central place in Gods purpose for all human life. Physical intercourse among Christians is not considered to be a necessary evil nor is it regarded simply as a means of bringing children in the world. Rather, it is will of the God. It is the sublimation of the energies of men and women in each other at biological, mental and religious level. The three precise objectives are: procreation, escape from fornication (sex relations without marriage) and mutual help and comfort. On the basis of these objects, the Christian marriage is defined as "contract between a man and a woman normally intended to be binding for life for the purpose of sexual union, mutual companionship and the established of a family".

The method of mate selection is quite like Hindus. It is either the parents or the parents and children together or the boys and girls themselves who play their part in the settlement of marriage. The conditions remain that it should not be from blood relations, should be matching the status of the family, education, character, qualities and the physical fitness. The questions of consanguinity and affinity do play its role as in the Hindus. There is no such thing as preferred persons for marriage in Christians. After the selection of the partner, betrothal ceremony is performing at the bride's house where the boy gives a ring to the girl. Occasionally the girl also gives a ring to the boy in exchange. This is, in fact, the engagement ceremony which may be performed privately or more ceremonially.

After the engagement, the formalities to be fulfilled include: producing a certificate of church membership, a certificate of character and submitting an application for marriage in the church three weeks before the due date. The church priest then invites the objections against the marriage. The marriage day is fixed, if no objection is received in a specified period.

On the marriage day, the wedding takes place in the church of which the girl happens to be the member. The priest asks the groom and the bride whether they accept each other as wife and husband and when they give their consent, he solemnizes the marriage by asking the couple to declare in the presence of the witnesses that "I (A.B.), in the presence of the Almighty God and in the name of our Lord Jesus Christ, do take thee (C.D.), to be my lawful wedded wife/husband".

The Christian practice monogamy, while polygamy and polyandry are strictly prohibited. The Indian Christian Marriage Act, 1872, amended in 1891, 1903, 1911, 1920 and 1928 covers all marriage aspects like who is to perform marriage, the place where it is to be performed (between 06:00 AM, and 07:00 PM), the minimum age of the boy and the girl at the time of marriage, and the condition(s) under which it is to be performed (the marriage partners should not have a living spouse at the time of marriage). The Christian practice divorce too, though the church does not appreciate it. The Indian Divorce Act, 1869 refers to the conditions under which the divorce may be obtained. It covers dissolution of marriage, declaring marriage null and void, decree of judicial separation, protection order and restitution of conjugal rights.

The marriage may be declared null and void on the grounds of close blood relationship between husband and wife, husband's impotency, insanity of the partner at the time of marriage, and bigamy. The judicial separation may be obtained on grounds of adultery and cruelty.

There is no practice of dower or dowry among Christians. Remarriage of the widows is not only accepted but encouraged. It may, thus, be concluded that the Christian marriage is not a sacrament like that of Hindu marriage. It is a contract between a man and a woman in which there is lower stress on the role of sex but greater on mutual help and companionship. The institution of family and kinship do exist among Christians. They normally have smaller family units of just parents and minor children because there is a tendency of starting the family afresh after the marriage. It does not, however, mean that a Christian family is ignorant about or insensitive to its aging parents. Self-made or some institutional resources through the organization of Church or other missions and old-age homes are preferred to sustain the old age. Blood relationship and kinship is quite cherished in the Christian society as well.

Jains, Bauddhists and Zoroastrians (Parsis):

Jains: The Jains are quite a recognizable community in India. There are more than four million adherents of Jainism who form 0.48 percent of the total population. Apparently, the Jains have the same disposition as Hindus, and unless one comes closer to their social customs and institutions it would not be possible to separate them from the latter. The jains are divided into two sects, the white-robed Shvetambara and those wearing no clothes called Digambaras. The latter are generally monks who are confined to a monastery. The Jain Upasakas or lay worshippers are called Shravakas and Shravikas. They mainly hail from the business communities of India. There is no social stratification within the Jain community.

The Jain householders form an endogamous community. In Jain wedding ceremony, a grand public announcement is made of the purpose of the soon-to-be bride and groom supposed to live together for their entire life. Life is thought to be a gift to be shared and growing together pardoning each-other's faults. Although, marriage and raising the family are not compulsory to all the Jain

Shravakas, the children born of the wedlock would be the disciple of the Jainism only. Parents play measure role in the settlement of marriage and other wedding ceremonies. Selection of match is done by the word of mouth and normally it is done among known people of their community. Almost all the marriage rites for Jains are the same as for the Hindus. Lagan-Lekhan or fixing of the time of the marriage is an important occasion in Jains when a 'pooja' is performed at girl's house and relatives are invited. The Lagan-patrika is sent to the boy's house along with sweets or laddoos and there it is read out in the presence of relatives. This may, however, be performed in the form of modern day engagement ceremony. The boy also performs a 'Vinayakyantra pooja' at the time of 'sagai' wearing a traditional Jain headgear. The bride's brother then puts a 'tilak' on the forehead of the groom. Thus this ceremony is alike the custom of 'tilak' in Hindu communities. The usual custom of taking the 'barat' to bride's house and its reception there are the further steps towards wedding. The procession starts from a nearby Jain temple and the custom of 'Ghudhchadi' (the groom riding a she-horse) is very much cherished. The wedding rituals consist of ceremonies like 'Phere', 'Kanyavaran', 'Havan' and 'Granthi Bandhan' and taking of the seven vows presided over by a Jain priest. The groom finally brings the bride to his house along with his kith-n-kin.

Another noticeable feature of the Jain marriage is its performance in the day-time because the Jains are supposed to finish their evening meals by the dust. The Jain Munis have ruled, since wedding ceremonies organized in the evening involve extravaganza, on the contrary, the Jain marriages have to be on austere side hence it should be organized in day-time. Further, it is ruled that no exchange of money should take place in the manner of dowry or otherwise. The predominant law of exclusive vegetarianism in Jainism has also to prevail both in the word and deed in all the affairs of Jain. The family structure and kinship of a Jain householder are almost the same as are in the Hindus.

Buddhist: There is hardly any Buddhist community in the mainland of India at present. Whatever Indian Buddhist communities we know are confined to Leh and Laddakh region in Jammu and Kashmir and some pockets in the Himachal Pradesh and other Himalayan ranges. Hence, their social structure and customs have nothing to do with Buddhism apart from their association with Buddhism, its' symbols, idols etc. The social and cultural patterns are mainly regional, which may be understood more in the terms of 'Pahari' (hilly) regional or 'Lama' traditions. No social stratification is found within these regional Buddhist peoples. They are also endogamous communities being few in number as compared to vast majority of other communities in India. The communities now named as 'Neo-Buddhist' are definitely different from these traditional regional Buddhists because they are the product of new social movement in India. These Neo-Buddhist communities can still be found as practicing all the Hindu practices even after declaring their faith in Buddhism. As far as the practice of marriage among Lamas is concerned, their wedding ceremony is very conventional reflecting the pomp and glamour and serious observation of rituals. The foremost and the most important ritual amongst these Buddhists is the horoscope matching. It is groom's party who first takes the consent of the girl's family on some auspicious day decided over by the Lama. The betrothal ritual follows called the Chessian betrothal ceremony. The lama recites the prayers in the presence of the maternal uncle of the bride seated on a raised platform. Then a concoction called the madyam (a sort of drink considered to be a religious drink) is served to the guests. Next, the monk called Lama decides the auspicious day for the wedding in consultation with an astrologer.

In the early morning, the bride's and the groom's families arrive at the Buddhist temple. The groom's family is obliged to offer fruits, wine, traditional cake, tea, meat, and most important jewelry that the bride will be getting as dowry in six or nine trays (considered to be auspicious number). One of the trays also contain a pair of candles which are to be lit either by the bride and the groom or their parents. The tradition varies with places and countries. The lighting up of the two candles symbolizes the unification of the two families. The monk carries out the rites on the auspicious day for wedding. The couple and the assembly deliver a procession hymns from Vandana, Tisarana and Pancasila before a specially constructed shrine and the image of Lord Buddha. The candles and the incense sticks are lit before the image of Lord Buddha and flowers are offered in abundance. Next, the bride and the groom narrate the traditional undertakings as described in Siglovadda Sutta. A red paste is applied on the foreheads of the bride and the groom. The groom says the following words:

"Towards my wife I undertake to love and respect her, be kind and considerate, be faithful, delegate domestic management, present gifts to please her. The bride in response says: "Towards my husband I undertake to perform my household duties efficiently, be hospitable to my in-laws and friends of my husband, be faithful, protect and invest our earnings, discharge my responsibilities lovingly and fastidiously".

The wedding ceremony comes to an end with the recital of Mangal Sutta and Jayamangala Gatha as a blessing for the newlyweds. Thus a Buddhist marriage is very simple and does not include any complex ritual. It is based on faith and less on religion. It has two components. One is the Buddhist component and the other is non-Buddhist component. The Buddhist component includes offering prayers along with gifts to the monks and the image of Buddha. The non-Buddhist component is reflected in regional and folk traditions and customs observed by the couple and their families. The ritual of red paste is similar to Hindus. The bride's mark is created with the butt of a candle keeping in with the tradition of not even touching the lady.

Buddhist weddings in recent times have cut down on the complicated ceremonies involved. Monks also have a greater role as compared to previous times when they were forbidden. The twin forces of modernity and scientific knowledge have made their influence on Buddhist weddings as well. Though Buddhist wedding is quite informal but their structure has change extensively. Initially monks did not attend the wedding, as they had to be present during the funeral rites. Nowadays, the role of the monks in weddings has become quite reflective. Buddhist weddings are customary ceremonies and are essential part of Buddhist culture.

Zoroastrians or the Parsis: Parsis are a very tiny but effective community in India confined mainly to the states of Maharashtra and Gujarat. Being one of the oldest civilized communities of the world who has retained its identity even till today is exclusively an endogamous community. They are the fire-worshippers and practically none of their rituals are complete without the use of fire. A Parsi wedding is full of gaiety and enjoyments. The 'achoo meecho' (removing the evil eye) is performed before every single ceremony. The auspicious days to conduct weddings are either the first day of the month ('Hormazd Roe') or the twentieth day of the month ('Behram Roj'). It is believed that on 'Behram Roj' the angel of victory or 'Behram' presides over the ceremonies. Most Parsi weddings take place in the evening, a little after sunset. The pre wedding rituals or customs begin four days before the 'lagan' and performed by the family priest. Pre-wedding rituals are called Rupia Peravanu. This is the unofficial engagement when both families acknowledge and give their assent for the marriage. On the wedding day staircase, doorway and gate is decorated with beautiful decorative designs of rangoli.

According to the Zoroastrians the time immediately after sunset or very early in the morning is considered auspicious for marriage. For the marriage ceremony the bride dresses in her madhavate the white, ornate wedding sari given by her parents, while the groom wears the traditional Parsi dagli and feta a white kurta like garment and a blackcap. The Parsi lagan is called Achoo meecho, which takes place either at a baug or at an agiary (the fire temple). The priest showers rice on the couple as a mark of wedding. The officiating priests, two in number, recite what is known as the 'Paevandnameh' or 'ashirwaad' (blessing). This recital consists of admonitions, prayers and benedictions. Once the admonitions are over, the priests recite the 'benedictions' invoking the favour of virtues from the 'Yazatas' (angels). The next set of prayers in this wedding ceremony is made in the honour of the dear departed souls.

A Parsi family is known to be a disciplined family and all the members of the family give regard to family customs and prestige. One unique custom in the Parsis is their funeral rite in which the dead is neither cremated nor buried but put on a high platform in 'Towers of Silence' meant for its decay or to be devoured by the vultures.

CHAPTER IV

GLOBAL IMPACT ON INDIAN SOCIETY

To understand the meaning of the subject, one must keep in mind that human civilizations and cultures in the remote past developed independently and separately in their isolated regional/geographical settings as per their natural situations. The human mind has always been interacting and negotiating with its surroundings and developing its belief systems and social practices, so you come to know about various cultures of anteriority. Earlier, the contact between such cultures was meager and confined to some adventurous traders who were able to establish contact with distant areas, for example, you know about trade links even between the proto-historic Indus and its contemporary Mesopotamian civilizations. With the conquering of the alien regions and peoples by some ambitious leaders and the emergence of vast political empires, however, larger areas were knit together, which also opened the gates of cultural interaction and progress of synthesized cultures and civilizations, expansion of trade links, and so on, in broader areas.

Furthermore, with the emergence and progress of new religious movements, Buddhism, Christianity, and Islam in particular, a greater number of people came together under their shades of religious culture, widening the boundaries of humanity. Thus, humanity, at large, has always been aspiring for expanding and widening the area of its activities in harmony and peace, despite the experiences of conflicts and wars quite contrary to it. The movement of travelers and adventurers from one part of the world to the other in the past and the penning down of their travelogues for posterity was part of the same quest for humanity.

However, now you will know that globalization, along with modernization, is quite a new phenomenon, both economic and cultural, in various stages of progress of humanity, which has brought about almost a revolutionary impact on the societies of the world. Indian society, in particular, known to be bound by long traditions on the one hand and variously classified in economic terms on the other, is taking this impact in multiple ways. It refers to changes in social structure, marriage and family systems, new attitudes towards religious rites and practices, new occupational scenarios, changing standards of living, and new cultural patterns.

CHAPTER V

CONCEPTS AND NATURE OF GLOBALIZATION

Globalization has become popular since the last century in the context of international trade regulations. Philosophically, the concept of global humanity developed as early as Vedic times in India. The slogan of 'Vasudheva kutumbakam' and 'krinvanto vishvam Aryam' (Rigveda: IX. 63. 5) were such expressions meaning that 'all the people on the earth are a family' and 'the whole of the world should be Aryanized' (Acculturated) respectively. Later, religious movements in India and elsewhere also tended to bind the people of the whole world in an ethical knot in their own ways and limitations. However, globalization of the present age has some specific connotations and a different approach towards making people and cultures of the world come together for the progress of humanity at large. Globalization is the system of interaction among the countries of the world in order to develop the global economy. Globalization refers to the integration of economies and societies worldwide. It involves technological, economic, political, and cultural exchanges, made possible largely by advances in communication, transportation, and infrastructure.

While the horrible experiences of the two world wars in the twentieth century had made the world community wise enough to look for such effective organizations at the world level, which could bring about cultural and political harmony among nations, it was further felt that this could not be achieved without economic progress and the uplift of the standard of living of all communities in whichever corners and regions of the world. Hence, a new approach to fulfilling this objective was conceived and planned. Economic assistance programmes through world agencies such as the World Bank and a Consortium of Funds with the name International Monetary Fund (IMF) for different schemes of development, particularly in developing and underdeveloped nations on the one hand, and the regulation of trade between nations with the specification of items and their quantity and even its production through the World Trade Organization (WTO) became the major planks of this globalization. Thus, Globalization in the modern age does not simply mean the universalization or spread of any philosophy or ethics for the world community, but it claims to be an economic program intended to minimize the economic disparity among nations and communities.

In practice, however, it intended to devolve upon the developing and underdeveloped nations the responsibility of freeing or cutting down the duties on import of items from other nations, compulsory import of certain items in exchange of their items of export, etc., which is presently termed as the policy of liberalization. In this sense, globalization is virtually equivalent to economic liberalization, implying that trade barriers are opened at the national level. The direct entry of foreign funds and the operation of Multinational Companies in other nations' domains is an important feature of globalization. This has certainly encouraged the movement of goods and people alike at the global level. It also offers new opportunities in the service sector and the flow of money from one place to another. The broadening of trade links has furthered social and cultural contacts and has enhanced the standard of living for a class of people who are either managers and administrators, or a part of this system with their befitting skills and expertise. Globalization, along with modernization, is penetrating deep into the psyche of the people, particularly of the urban citizenry of countries in the areas of technical and vocational education, health care, sports, leisure, entertainment, and touring. However, the negative implications and impacts of globalization need to be examined separately.

CHAPTER VI

CONCEPT AND NATURE OF MODERNIZATION

When you start talking about modernization, an immediate thought comes to mind that it is a way of living with modern ideas and institutions as well as new means and technology. Modernization is often likened to Westernization, with the assumption that almost all new institutions and technology have been imported or adopted from the West in the modern age. Noted Sociologist M.N. Srinivas preferred the term 'Westernization' to modernization. Milton Singer (Traditional India: Structure and Change, Philadelphia, 1959), Yogendra Singh (Modernization of Indian Tradition, Jaipur, 1983), and some other sociologists prefer 'modernization' in place of 'Westernization'. Srinivas argues that the term" modernization' is subjective, while the term 'Westernization' is more objective (Seminar, 88, 1986:2). According to him, the concept of Westernization refers to "the changes in technology, institutions, ideology and values of a non-western society as a result of cultural contact with the western society for a long period" (Srinivas, Caste in Modern India and Other Essays, Bombay, 1962, p. 55; Social Changes in Modern India, Los Angles, 1966). Further, he suggests that, to some extent, Westernization has also been complimentary to the process of 'Sanskitization' (Acculturation) of the lower castes in India with the general access to new technology, democratic institutions and freedom of choice of social and religious rites. Because, Sanskritization in earlier days happened to be a social mechanism of assimilating various communities and clans into a broader canvas of Brahmanical culture, maintaining at the same time, the ritual distance between the brahmanas along with other higher castes and the lower castes, but the latter are now trying to catch up with them socially with the new tools of Westernization in their hands.

Modernization, however, has a wider meaning and many dimensions. Though it is not a philosophy or movement with a clearly articulated value system, it should be remembered that the modern era was initiated with the renaissance and reformation in Europe and elsewhere, which meant the revival of the spirit of reasoning and rationality. Historically, it implied that humanity had done away with this spirit in the Middle Ages, which was to be corrected with the change in circumstances. The process of change, of course, started appearing in the establishment of new political, administrative, economic, social, educational, technological, military, and so forth institutions. This is perceivable in the behavior of the individual, group, community, or society at large. It is perceivable in terms of food and clothing habits and the standard of living. This is reflected in the changes in social structure, marriage and kinship systems, religious rites, practices, and so on.

CHAPTER VII

IMPACT OF GLOBALIZATION & MODERNIZATION ON INDIA

The impact of Globalization and Modernization on Indian society is both apparent and fundamental. It has to be first examined in terms of the changes in the social structure and marriage and family systems, as well as religious attitudes and practices of different shades.

Social Changes: Caste, Class, Marriage and Family:

At the social structural level, there is a decline in the traditional principle of ascribed status and role to achieve status and role. The castes in India were theoretically and traditionally bracketed with the fourfold division and the hierarchy of the varnas Brahmanas, Kshatriyas, Vaishyas, and Shudres, as well as a fifth known as ati-Shudras or untouchables. Since the hierarchy of the castes and discrimination based on this theory has now been totally rejected in the modern democratic constitution of India, new vistas of structural social change have been opened. The democratic system of achieving political power based on numerical support, affirmative action programs on the part of the government, and special provisions for the uplift of the deprived or low sections of society, modern technology, institutions, new occupations and nature of services, and new means of earning bread and accumulation of wealth, banking system, etc. are various other factors contributing to structural social change pertaining to the caste and class structure of Indian society.

A unique feature of modernization in India is that it is being carried forward through adaptive changes in traditional structures rather than structural dissociation or breakdown. The occupations practiced by castes, their diet, and the customs they observe, determine their status in the hierarchy. Thus, practicing an occupation such as tanning, butchery, or handling a toddy puts the caste in a low position. Eating beef, fish, and mutton is considered defiling. Offering animal sacrifices to deities is viewed as a lower practice than offering fruit and flowers. As such, castes following these customs, diet habits, etc., adopt the life of brahmanas to achieve a higher status in the caste hierarchy. Though theoretically forbidden, this is the movement of a low caste upward in the social structure of a generation or two. This, in his view, is now also linked to westernization, which furthers these possibilities.

Another dimension of structural change is the rejection of old values and social conditions. In this context, it may be pointed out that the formation and settlement of castes in earlier times was related to the factors and scope of mobility and non-mobility of occupations and people under the hegemony of traditional priestly and political powers. The castes continued to remain enclosed groups in a self-sustaining closed economy of rural or village settings, and this number increased on the basis of little or more distinctions of occupation, technique, food and dress habits, rites and customs, regions, etc. The urban impact, on the other hand, has always been negative to calcification of castes. Even if there is no rejection of older values and systems, people tend to move away from them in urban settings. Traditional norms and restrictions on inter-dining and inter-caste marriages among different caste people are rapidly diluting in big cities. Modernization or Westernization with globalization has changed the traditional caste structure with the formation of new social classes.

Restriction on inter-dining is almost a thing of the past, even in smaller cities. Inter-caste and even inter-religious marriages no longer invite that wrath on the part of parents and the related community at home if solemnized between capable youths in big cities. A new class of professionals, administrators, managers, and persons in other service sectors is rapidly emerging with the advent of multinational companies (MNCs), the opening up of new sectors of service, and the establishment of new institutions and organizations such as NGOs. A new compact of people is in the making of their respective organizations based on the equality of their standard of living. This is quite explainable in terms of the faster growth rate of middle classes of different grades in India over the last two to three decades, which is now around 40 percent of the large Indian population.

The impact of Globalization and Modernization on institutions of marriage and family are also perceivable particularly in the urban life. Though the marriage rites and general conditions of marriage remain the same as per regional customs even in the cities, but some new ways of celebrating the occasions have come into practice. These are manifest in performance of engagement and marriage ceremonies at different venues, normally hotels or lawns, than at the house of groom or bride. New cuisines go on adding to the throwing of dinner at the occasion. Sometimes these are organized jointly by both the parties.

As far as the practice of dowry is concerned, though it is prohibited by law, it has taken the form of gifts depending upon individual attitude of the parties, as the greed for acquiring more and more resources of living and property by any means has also developed as a result of modernization. Marriage as a compulsory institution is also being questioned by a few ultra modern persons for their increasing claims of individual freedom. Even the educated and self-dependent girls in the cities sometimes tend to prefer unmarried life lest their individual personality not be compromised. An extreme position is now being taken in 'live-in-relationship'. Separation and divorce among couples are also becoming more acceptable in the society. It is, however, a matter of debate for the social scientists whether all this should be taken as positive or negative impacts of modernization.

The family system was also affected. The traditional system of joint families, when at least two to three generations are used to living together in an agricultural or rural setting, is rapidly breaking in urban areas. Since the new nature of occupations and services is taking the people off to distant places within and outside the country away from their native places, and even the persons in the first generation are not able to live together because of their engagement at different places, a general tendency is towards the nuclear family, which means living just the couple and their children until the latter are dependent and not married. The cost of education for the children and the growing standard of living are also pushing such nuclear families to keep away from the joint responsibilities of the families. The urban elite are fast adopting the concept of having only one or two children.

A fallout effect of modernization may be seen in the tendency of sex detection of the child with the help of new medical techniques before its birth in order to get at least one male child among couples, particularly in cities. This is because a male child in Indian society is considered necessary for the funeral rites of parents. In addition, a female child is looked upon as a burden and a cause and source of insecurity, drawing away from family resources and assets by a number of parents. However, the same attitude towards a daughter or a girl is not met with everyone, and you may find persons or families contrary to this thought cherishing, at the same time, the birth and upbringing of a daughter in their utmost capacity in this modern age.

The above feature of the nuclear family, however, is further depriving future families of many kinds of kinships, as there could be no real brother or sister, daughter and son, sala and sali (wife's brother and sister), jija (sister's husband), bua and phupha (father's sister and her husband) and chacha and chachi (father's brother and his wife), mama and mami (mother's brother and his wife), mausi and mausa (mother's sister and her husband), and the like relations to many persons that have long remained the mainstay of the Indian family system. With the dilution of family bonds and growing self-centeredness, the family structure, particularly in urban India, has been badly affected and seems to be heading towards Western systems of family.

Yet, many traditional customs of families are still prevalent in different regions of the country, and different communities in India have taken the effect of or adopted new ideas, institutions, and technology in a manner suitable to their traditions. Hence, the impact of Globalization and

Modernization in India varies from community to community and region to region, which is also related to the pace of infiltration of modern systems and urbanization of the areas.

Impacts on Religious Rites and Practices:

The impact of Globalization and Modernization on the religious life of the people in India is worth noting, considering that Indian society is religiously minded. You may find the present religious scenario in India confusing. Apparently, there is a greater tendency to visit religious shrines and temples in the deities.

Numerically, pilgrimage is growing leaps and bound with the facilities of transport and communication, and even many in the younger generation are fascinated to go around for pilgrimage sake. Individual devotees and group processions of Kanvariyas and others can be seen rushing to different religious spots and shrines of saints and gurus during prescribed or popular seasons.

Religious fairs and festivals such as Kumbha melas, Deewali, Dashera, Chhatha Puja, Durga Puja, and Ganesh Mahotsava are now being organized with more gaiety, and an increasing number of people are being assembled on such occasions. Many other religious programs of mass assemblage are also becoming popular with new systems of advertisement, such as electronic and print media. A number of new shrines and temples with gorgeous structures are emerging all around the country, and older sites are being renovated. Then, you see a mushroom growth of new babas and swamis preaching around religious ethics, and some of them even display their magical and mysterious powers and suggest curious means and ways to their followers to get rid of their miseries or fulfilling some of their desires and ambitions.

This may indicate a growing indulgence of the peoples in religious affairs, but sociologically it may be understood as a result of new facilities of transport, communication, and advertisement of the programmes on one side, and a growing sense of insecurity and frustration, stress, and challenges of living and work in the modern age on the other, along with the multiplying population in the country.

Given the above scenario of the religious life of Indian people, it is also important to note the other side of religious practices. Traditionally, a number of religious rites were to be performed by individuals privately as their daily rites or as special rites under the supervision of a priest in Hindus. This practice is now becoming unpopular in big cities with lifestyle changes and the lack of availability of exclusive priests in the vicinity. Moreover, it appears to be difficult to visit a shrine or temple or to join a religious gathering that more often serves other purposes of outing, shopping, etc. than engaging oneself in daily rites and rituals, as well as bothering about ethical commitments of the religion. This can be taken as a practical impact of the new economic systems and urban culture of the modern age.

Occupational Changes:

As modernization implied revolutionary changes in scientific information and technology, traditional occupational structures were bound to be replaced by new occupations. College trained engineers working in large industrial settings and having higher social status due to their better standard of living with their higher source of income started challenging the existence of traditional artisans and craftsmen with lower social status and lower source of income. Although some technological aid also went into traditional craftsmanship alongside the new demands of the market, which somewhat helped raise the economic status of these artisans and craftsmen for some time, this too appeared to be losing with total automation of the manufacturing of goods in the industrial sector. The traditional guilds of artisans gave way to the industrial groups. There is a demand for trained managers to run the industry.

A new class of administrators as well as the 'babus' (office assistants) for conducting and assisting the work in newly formed institutions and organizations also came into existence both in the public and private sector. A big change was also visible in health sector, where again the college trained medical graduates started taking over the traditional 'vaidya' and 'hakim' with medicines of quick relief and their more organized nursing homes. Education was another sector that experienced sea change in its nature and form of imparting knowledge and training. New types of schools, colleges and universities required new kind of teachers in the place of traditional 'pathashalas' and 'madarsas' run by traditional individual teachers.

The defense organization of the new nation and the need for the police force to maintain internal law and order also opened avenues for new types of services. A host of other avenues for skilled and non-skilled workers was opened with the building of new infrastructure in the areas of transport, such as roads, railways, waterways, and aviation, and construction of office and institutional buildings and residential colonies in both the public and private sectors.

Changes in occupational structure started occurring even more rapidly with further technological development in space, satellite, and software technology, and revolution in information technology, along with the arrival of multinational companies, particularly with globalization and liberalization. Even the basic sectors of production, such as agriculture and base industries, have started experiencing an inflow of professionals with new technological knowhow. Both inland and foreign trade and new business organizations have started looking for personnel with more advanced managerial skills and expertise. There is a demand for professionally qualified persons. A large number of large industrial groups and public organizations have developed their own Research and Development (R&D) wings to explore the possibilities of enhancing the quality and variety of their products and marketing. Electronics and Computer operations, education and health, hospitality and tourism, food and beverage, sports, and defense are some of the main areas that draw people to cities and organizations offering newer types of occupations. A big thrust is on towards professional and vocational education and training, which has also furthered the establishment of such centers in cities, universities, and colleges, requiring specialized teachers of the trade at the same time. Thus, a new occupational structure is bringing about significant changes in the traditional Indian social system.

CHAPTER VIII

STANDARD OF LIVING

The biggest change as a result of Globalization and Modernization can be observed in the standard of living of people. The new technology has tremendously lured people to the exploitation of nature and natural resources to fulfill their needs and avail luxuries. As far as India is concerned, there is a serious problem of space for shelters for all with the swelling population in urban centers. While only a small number of people are capable of affording large bungalows and maintaining their private lawns and gardens, there is a great rush for flats in multistoried buildings, even in smaller cities and cabal towns. Living in a flat and the societies organized for that is itself a new experience for people. Such societies have come up as smaller townships in their right, having all the essential facilities of a market, nursing home or a physician, gym, swimming pools, sports arena, library, club house, etc., in a secure and protected environment.

Urban Home: Both Globalization and Modernization have provided a new look at the homes of individual families with the availability of a variety of goods and fanciful things in the market, including foreign items. Starting from household furniture, wardrobes, mats, carpets, tiles, television, computer, music and sound systems, refrigerator, bathroom geezers and tubs and sanitary fittings, washing machines, desert coolers, air conditioners, a modular kitchen, tens and hundreds of electronic gadgets and appliances for it, and other utility and luxury items, a modern home may now be found equipped with so many things depending on the resources of income of a person or a family. Keeping one's own means of transport, like two wheelers and cars or vans, even both of it and more if possible, is another addition to this standard of living. Carrying one or more cell phones has also become the order of day, even for those who are unable to afford all the above-mentioned luxuries. 'Live simply and think highly' is no more the ethic of life for the people of this new era.

Food Habits: Despite carrying on their traditional food habits and banking upon their family staple food, a modern Indian family ought to adventure in a variety of new cuisines of different regions, as well as continental. This includes South Indian snacks and Chinese, Italian, and French dishes. Packed and half-ready food materials readily available in the market are a useful source for such experiments at home. Electrical and electronic gadgets such as refrigerators, ovens, microwaves, and mixing appliances. New dining decorations and decorums and the use of fancy cutlery have further added to the gaiety of the feeding habits of urban Indians. A big trend of relishing fast food or junk food on the roadside and going to restaurants and hotels for eating has also developed in the cities.

Dress Habits: As far as the dress habits of the Indians in the present are concerned, it has already been changing ever since the rule of Britain in India. It was earlier mainly related to the introduction of new systems of education and work in the colonial period, which, of course, amounted to the Westernization of Indian systems. Men in the cities quickly adopted the Western styles of trousers, shirts, and coats, whereas the women in India were slow to adopt Western dress, because there was almost no scope for a woman to go for her education and work or to any social place independent of men even in the cities. However, with the growing opportunities for her movement, encouragement of women's education, and growing acceptance of a working woman in the upper castes and middle class of Indian society, there has been a great change in the dressing and clothing of women, at least in the cities. The dresses are not simply confined to Western adoptions, but now it is a global phenomenon and fashions may arrive from any part of the world, suiting the psyche of change and glamour, even for a short time. The dress designers and companies sell their products through large-scale advertisements and fashion shows. So much so that you have now entered the era of designer attire and clothing in large cities.

Education of Children: The Children's education has become a big issue for parents today. Although some big efforts are going into reorganizing the public education system and education of children is being made compulsory, due to deterioration and lack of public commitment to the schooling and education of children at the ground level, there is a great desperation in finding good schools for children. Obviously, there is a mushroom growth in schools and colleges in the private sector, which are charging high fees for their maintenance. Parents are likely to send their children to the best of such schools and colleges in their vicinity or even to distant places, to some foreign countries like Australia, England, and the U.S. as well, as per their resources, with the objective of making them compete with the demands of the new world. Besides regular schooling, there is also a big trend of sending children to attend coaching classes for some particular standard or for clearing some entrance and competitive examinations. These coaching centers or institutes again demand handsome fees for coaching depending on the reputation of their center, which is affordable by not many. It has also become a status symbol for parents as to what type and level of education they can afford their children. The introduction of computers and the revolutionary growth of information technology are significantly changing modes of learning. Online courses on Internet and websites have offered access to so many new things for students as well as professionals.

Health Care: A Considerable attention has been paid to health care in this age of globalization. Many business agencies and social organizations are out of campaigning for maintaining good health. Public shows of yoga and other exercises and displays of yoga, aerobics, etc., as well as medical counseling on television shows, are all part of this campaign, which, of course, is also a new area of medical business. The affluent class of society is out to keep the apparatus for exercise, such as trade machines, at home. The richer class even has its own private gym and swimming pool. Otherwise, a good number of people of all age groups in big cities tend to join gym, health, yoga clubs, and youths ought to join sports arenas and stadiums, swimming pools, and golf clubs in their vicinity. Big business enterprises and offices are now offering gym facilities to their workers to relax their muscles as a respite from their tidy office work. Walking, running, and laughing exercises in the morning and evening have become common features of urban life. Then, you may also find people concerned more about their regular medical check-ups in order to prevent any ailment or to get it cured at the initial level, if detected. There are specialized doctors and nursing homes for general and specific ailments or diseases. Maternity homes are now on the order of the day, and both rich and common people now prefer to use these homes for childbirth and care.

Market and Malls: The talk about a new standard of living will be incomplete if you miss the most common feature of shopping in the markets, both in the smaller towns and big cities. It is an age of business and people are lured to buy utility and fashion items all the time. Big departmental stores and showrooms of different products have already made their mark alongside the petty retail shops in the market. A new culture of Mall has developed in big cities that offers fanciful items and entertainment to customers or visitors. A number of big malls are coming up in big cities and even in cabal towns where people flock in for everything fashionable they wish to avail.

CHAPTER IX

CULTURAL IMPACTS

In India, people live in both their traditional culture and modern lifestyle. Many new colors have been added to traditional fairs and festivals as a result of globalization and modernization. Apart from popularly known festivals of Diwali, Durga Puja and Navaratra, Holi, Lohri, Pongal, Ganeshotsava, Makar Shankranti, Eid, Baquareid, Muharram and Shab-e-Baraat, Guru Nanak Jayanti, Christmas, Ishtar and Goa Carnival, Buddha Purnima and Navaroj, a number of old and new fairs and festivals are celebrated in different states of India all around the year.

To name a few in addition to the above mentioned festivals you may refer to Badri-Kedar festival, Ganga festival, and International Yoga Week at Rishikesh in Uttarakhand; Shiva Ratri, Ganga Mahotsav, Deva Deepawali, Lolark Chhatha, Buddhava Mangal and Mahamoorkha Sammelan on Ganga ghats at Varanasi, and Buddha Mahotsav at Saranath, and daily Ganga Arti both at Varanasi and Hardwar; Taj Mahotsav at Agra and Avadh or Lucknow Mahotsav, Vrindavan Shardotsav, Hariyali Teej in Haryana; Baba Bakla, Chhapar Mela, Harballah, Sangeet Sammelan and Mukutsar Maghi fair in Punjab; Chait, Flaich or Oo-Khyang, Ghantul festival, Maghi, Phagli, Pauri Yatra, Tushimig, Bala Sundari fair, Chhatrari fair, Dhoogri fair, Gaddi fair and Gugga fair in Himachal Pradesh; Hemis festival, Mansar festival and Mei Lozar in Jammu and Kashmir; Mahamoorkh Sammelan in Chandigarh and Festival of Garden (earlier known as Rose Festival) both at Chandigarh and New Delhi; Mango festival, Phool Waloon ki Sair, International Kite festival and National Day celebrations at New Delhi; Bohag Bihu, Magh Bihu, Kangali Bihu, Ali-Ali Ligno festival, Amsbubashi Mela (Kamakhya shrine) and Tea festival in Assam; Annueno Torgia, Nyokam, Mopin, Tamladu Reh and Boori-Boot in Arunachal Pradesh; Cheiraoba, Chumpha, Ganga-Ngai, Keikru Hitongba, Kut, Lal Haroba, Vaoshang and Ningol Chakouba in Manipur; Behdiengkhlam, Ka Pamblang Nongkrem, Shad Sukmynsiem and Wangala in Meghalaya; Chapchar Kut, Mimkut and Pawl Kut in Mizoram; Amongmong, Aoling, Metemneo, Minakut Moatsu, Monyu, Ngada, Nga-Ngai, Naknyulum, Pikhuchak, Sekrenyi, Tokhu Emong, Tsokum, Tsungremmong and Tulmuni-Yemshe in Nagaland; Pous Sankranti festival, Garia and Gajan Puja, Ashokastami, Kharchi Puja, Orange and Tourism festival in Tripura; Benden Khlam, Drupka Teeshi, Guthor Chaam, Losar, Losoong, Pang Lhausol, Saga Dawa, Shad Suk Mynsiem and Tse-Chuu Chham in Sikkim; Indra Puja, Jhapan, Kali Puja in West Bengal; Dala Chhatha, Malamasa Mela, Pitrapaksha Tarpan at Gaya, Sonepur Mela (Asia's biggest Cattle fair) in Bihar; Konark Dance Festival, Makar Mela, Magha Mela, Dola or Holi, Taratarini Mela, Chaitra Parba, Rath Yatra, Rajrani Festival, Ashokastami in Orissa; Akhil Bhartiya Kalidas Samaroh at Ujjain, Ameer Khan Festival at Indore, Dhrupad Samaroh at Bhopal and a festival of dance at Khajuraho in Madhya Pradesh; Bhai Dooj, Camel Festival at Jaisalmer, Pushkar Mela at Ajmer and Shilpagram Crafts Mela in Rajasthan; Danga Darbar festival, Modhera Dance Festival, Ambaji Fair, Chitra Vichitra Fair, Shamiaji Fair, Tarnetar Fair and Vasutha no Melo in Gujarat; Banganga festival, Narali Pournima and Vithoba festivals in Maharashtra; International Sea Food Festival, Feast of St. Xavier, Shigmo and International Film

Festival in Goa; Ashtabhandhana, Batkamma, Bonalu and Krishna Pushkaram in Andhra Pradesh; Navarasapur-Paltadakkal and Coorg Festival in Karnataka; Mahabalipuram Dance Festival, Chittarai Festival and Ooty Summer Festival in Tamil Nadu; Maquerade and Sani Peyarchi in Puducherry, and Arat Festival, Boat Race and the Great Elephant March in Kerala.

Many of these fairs and festivals are traditionally celebrated earlier than the age of modernization, but they have gained in stature and dimension due to the ever-growing participation of people with newer items and programs being added to it in their celebration. Besides, you come across a number of secular fairs and festivals have been added to the list, such as Craft Melas, Music and Dance festivals, Mahamoorkh Sammelan (festivals of jest, mockery, and caricature), flower festivals and Feasts and Fates, Book Fairs, Industrial and Agricultural Fairs, and seminars and conferences organized periodically or scheduled as per need and occasions.

Both Classical and folk music and dance traditions are presented in organized stages, and the growing impact of Western music and dance styles is also visible, particularly in big cities with the organization of big music and dance shows of celebrated Western singers and dancers from outside and within India. Film Festivals also take the limelight due to the ever-widening attraction for films in the new generation. This clearly speaks to the cultural life of the people in present-day India.

Many institutions and organizations have come into existence in the fields of art, music, dance, and drama, such as Sangeet Evam Nritya Academy and Prayag Sangeet Sammelan, which promote the art skills of individuals and groups. Some national-level awards of high repute are offered to people excelling in this field.

Most of the time, people are resigned and confined to their homes after a long and strenuous schedule of their job listening to music, watching television at home, and enjoying home theatres individually or with their family members and friends. Some indulge in their hobbies, such as painting, music, dance, and writing, which are now finding better opportunities for public displays. People tend to go outing to parks or picnic spots on weak ends and Sundays or on holidays. While attending public theatres, musical concerts and dance shows, social and religious discourses, visiting paintings, and art galleries is a cultural feature of the intellectual elite of the city, watching movies in Multiplexes and other cinema halls, and watching big national and international meetings and events like crickets are some of the most common entertainments of the people in the cities. Visiting a Race course and watching car rallies are some specific tastes, whereas attending periodic and occasional public fairs and festivals is the most common feature of the cultural life of the people.

Finally, apart from the growing rush in the traditional pilgrimage discussed above, travel and tour to different sites of historical, cultural, and natural importance and visit and stay at places and sites of sea, hill or water sports, hill stations in summers or winters in addition to the swelling taste of pilgrimages make up most of the cultural activities of the people in the present day. Tourism is gaining importance and efforts are being made, both at the public and private levels, to organize it in a greater way. Travel organizations, agencies, hotels, and tour operators are putting their stakes into the hospitality business and service sector. Companies offer handsome packages to lure people into going around within and outside India.

CHAPTER X

Learning from this book (summary)

In this book you learnt about the individual and general social customs, courtesies and obligations as envisaged in relevant scriptures and traditions of different religious communities. You found that a Hindu as an individual is loaded with a lot of family and social responsibilities and all his acts from birth to death are targeted to a purpose towards the humanity and the nature. You learnt that all the communities have some social duties to perform in the form of charities or otherwise. They have a number of occasions to interact and some festivals are organized at inter-communal level.

Then you have been told about the social institutions of major religious communities. The Caste-system in the Hindus and social classes of different nature in the Muslims, Sikhs and Christians has come to notice.

The institution of marriage is the most attractive feature of the social system. In the Hindus it has religious overtone as all other activities. In the Muslims it is a social contract between man and woman. In the Christians it is beginning of the companionship.

Thus, in this book, you first explained the concept and nature of the two words, Globalization and Modernization. While Globalization in the present sense refers to cross-geographical and cross-national intellectual and economic activities with regard to ideas and knowledge, technology, and services, as well as production, trade, and cultural exchanges and relationships at the global level, modernization implies change in ideas and attitudes, creation and establishment of new institutions, and change in the standard of living of the people as a whole. You could know how the traditional caste structure in India has been affected and a new class of administrators, managers, professionals, etc. has developed in the present Indian society, what new trends have developed with regard to marriage and family systems, and how the families are becoming increasingly nuclear in the urban setting, with an emphasis on individualism. How kinship bonds are affected by the trend of smaller families. Then you could also know about the new scenario of religious life of the people, as you were explained that religious activities in India seem to be expanding in dimension, but individual ethics and private religious rites appear to be declining due to changes in lifestyle.

Globalization and Modernization have a significant impact on the upcoming expansion of the service sector with regard to occupations. So, you have found that the occupations are not confined to certain sectors of production and distribution, but almost an army of professional experts, managers, and office assistants is required to run national and international affairs and business and to serve and cater to the ever-growing needs of society. You have also found that a great change has occurred in the standard of living of the people, particularly in cities with the availability of a host of new articles and appliances and access to new sources of leisure and luxury as per your pocket. The cultural life of people is also changing with the addition of new colors. Better scope and opportunities to showcase and display one's art and individual group aspirations have arisen. All of this makes for the impact of Globalization and Modernization on the Indian society.

The effects of globalization on Indian society and culture are as follows:

Family Structure and Role of Women in Family: The joint family which had been the basis of traditional Indian families has undergone serious changes. Those residing in the metropolitan cities in the small flat culture prefer nuclear families. We have lost the persistence to get balanced into the joint family, assimilating the experiences of the older folks and getting the youthful ones raised under the shadow of their grandparents. Kids have begun treating grandparents like visitors or guests, and such upbringing of children is one of the principle reasons of expanding old-age homes, as those youngsters think about their own parents as burden in their adulthood. Although women and men are equal before the law and therefore the trend toward gender equality has been noticeable, women and men still occupy distinct functions in Indian society. Woman's role within the society is usually to perform family and household related activities. However, with the change in time men and women are gaining equal right to education, to earn, and to articulate.

Marriage System and Values: Additionally, marriages in comparison to earlier times have lost their values and morality. It is especially obvious from the expanding number of separation cases and extra-marital affairs reported every now and then. Marriage used to be considered as bonding of souls which will be connected even after the demise of the partners; yet today marriage resembles an expert bond or a purported pledge to share existence without bargaining their self-interests. Traditional ways of arranged marriages by the parents consent has been replaced by marriage by own liking by the partners. The sense of self factor into the Indian youth is again a result of globalization.

Infidelity: Both the genders had to maintain a distance as much as possible, with numerous confinements and impediments for a very long time in our culture and way of life. With the rise of globalization and western culture, youth have begun mixing up well with each other. The cordial approach and the mingling are apparent. The aggregate breakout of restrictions has tainted the Indian mentality, playing up with the physical relationship. A new type of relationship concepts namely live-in-relationship has emerged. Additionally the exaggerated cases of sexual offense cases are the results of the perverted mind that are very much the values considerably alien to our mother culture.

Festivals and Social Values: We have the included values of treating the guests as God, warm-hearted welcoming, greeting elders with due respect and a celebrating every small festival with great colour of enjoyment and togetherness. Such a wide gathering with full shade and light can barely be seen today. Individuals have profoundly limited themselves in social collaboration. The relation in present generation is exceptionally conciliatory thinking about the money related status and riches. We are losing our social morals and ideals and happy moments of harmony and peace. The present age generation is glad observing Valentine's Day and friendship day than Holi and Diwali. Traditionally namaste, namaskar or touching of feet of elders is a common way of greeting in the Indian subcontinent. But in modern times 'Hi', 'Hello' is used to greet people in place of Namaskar. Food,

Clothing and Dialect: Indian food, attire and dialects are different in different states. The food varies in its taste having its own nutrient values and each region is specific and rich in its resto rative arrangements with the home cures. Indeed, even the attire fluctuates in various states which are especially specific in keeping up the nobility of lady. The various cuisines from different places throughout the world however have distinctive flavours to include; still the food ingredients that have inflicted with much popularity are the junk food items which have increased the health disorders in the country. Again, the dressing like the clothes for the males are an unseemly comfortable for the India n climate. The female dresses are again a diversion to the tainted minds. Indeed, even the Indians are not in favour of promoting their mother tongue or our national language. Rather, the adolescent today view it as a disgraceful condition to talk in their national dialect Hindi. The manner in which the foreign languages are getting common in India like the French, German and Spanish, right from the school level, gives the examples of the amount of significance we give to Indian dialects and languages in co ntrast with the remote ones.

Work and Agricultural Sector: India was overwhelmingly an agriculture based nation. With the propelled globalization and springing up of MNCs, the farming and agriculture has lost its prime importance in India. Agriculture science has minimal concentration among the youths who consider cultivating as a despicable calling. We are losing our wellbeing and our status and gradually getting to the period of financial servitude because of these MNCs.

Education Sector: There are significant effects in academic sector because of globalisation like higher literacy rate and foreign universities collaborating with different Indian universities. The Indian academic system faces challenges of globalization through info-technology although it offers opportunities to evolve new paradigms shifts in developmental education. Globalization promotes new tools and techniques such as E-learning, flexible learning, distance education programs and overseas training programs.

Indian Business Culture: The foreign culture has both constructive and contrary impact on individuals and business firms. New ways of thinking and working has developed leading to higher efficiency. Indian organizations have embraced international accounting standards, Just-in-time and other more effective methods of stock control, flextime and new practices of human asset administration, social duty and business morals thoughts, improvement in corporate governance practices, customer relationship management practices, inflow of outside assets and healthy competition with foreign products. The business area in India is profoundly encouraging in the present situation. The effect of globalization has changed the business system in India in terms of psychology, approach, innovation, attitude, work culture and so on.

As a consequence of globalization Indian industries are adapting themselves to newer challenges and taking benefit from the new and better opportunities making their business all the more profitable with prospects of future growth. The colossal populace of India has made a huge unsaturated market of customers. This is one reason why worldwide organizations are particularly inspired in doing business in India. In the post globalization period this degree has expanded enormously for worldwide multinational organizations as Government of India has likewise played an exceptionally essential and steady part in this regard through changed liberalized strategies and administrative structure. A few situations that have arisen in India post liberalization era are as follows: urbanization and people of rural areas preferring to shift to urban areas, agriculture workers shifting to industry sector, trade market getting opened, boom in international import and export, big open saturated market for products, a growing market for high quality and low price product, gradual increase of organized retail chain, growing range of merger and acquisitions and lucid license policies for overseas multinational corporation. High growth rate is showing economic prosperity in India. Indian market leaders are going global.

Space, Science and Technology: India has created a distinct place in the field of space science and technology viz. launch services, earth observation, communication & navigation and application of space technology for national development. Today, India stands one amongst the top six space faring nations in the world. The areas that are benefitted/ seemingly to be benefitted with the use of space technology and its applications embrace – resource monitoring, weather forecasting, telecommunication, broadcasting, rural connectivity, health & education, governance, disaster management support, location based services, space commerce together with host of social applications.

Conclusion: India is obtaining a worldwide recognition and slowly moving towards to become a significant economic and political strength. Market economic policies are spreading around the world, with greater privatization and liberalization than in earlier decades. Globalization has resulted in growing global markets in services. People can now execute trade services globally -- from medical advice to software writing to data processing that could never really be traded before. India features a consumer base of 1.14 billion people. The mobile subscriber base has grown up from 0.3 Million in 1996 to over 250 million currently. In the cities Internet facility is everywhere. Extension of internet facilities has extended even to rural areas. Global food chain /restaurants have already found a large market within the urban areas of India. Lavish multiplex movie halls, big shopping malls and high rise residential buildings are seen in every city. Software Industries and telecommunication sectors are enjoying a tremendous boost in India. Bollywood movies are distributed and accepted worldwide. Programming and software Industries, telecommunications and media segments are getting benefits out of a gigantic lift of this sector in India. Entertainment sector in India has made a significant place for itself in the global market. Indian television channels and serials are watched and liked by people of different countries all over the world. New technologies are being used in agriculture sector resulting in improved yield of crops. Though the development is progressing rapidly, still many basic problems like prevailing poverty in rural areas, menace of corruption and instability of the government in the political arena are a cause of concern and steps should be taken to bring solution to such problems so as to reap the benefits of globalization in the best possible manner.

The Author

Dr. Anshumali Pandey is a renowned & reliable name in the field of Education, Hospitality, Tourism and Tribal Food. He is a Teacher and Chef by profession, and also an Author, a Business Auditor, and an avid culinary traveller to the Indian Sub continental hinterlands. Dr. Anshumali Pandey is a Hospitality Educator (PhD) who specialises in Higher Education, Office Administration, Pay roll, HR, Labour Laws, Audit, and Procurement & Tender Process. He is an Author with 67 Publications consisting of 49 Books and 3 short stories.

His contribution and research in the field of Tribal Food, Tribal Tourism, Forest Tourism and Village Tourism in the form of research papers have brought several laurels to him. In 2018 the Ministry of Tourism, Govt of Indian duly recognised all this and awarded him with a National Appreciation certificate and memento.

The books written by **Dr Anshumali Pandey** are essentially a banquet arising from an experience of over 25 years of Professional life and have boiled down to crisp and accurate writing on his favourite subjects. Hospitality Sector champion requires to be a specialist in many fields and Dr Pandey is one of them. His knowledge is evident from the spectrum of subjects which he has chosen for his books so far, which ranges from being a specialist chef, to Master of Human resources, to Education and to love for children, and topped with Spirituality. For more than two decades Dr Pandey has lived with his family in Western India in general and the Tribal belt of the union territory of Dadra & Nagar Haveli in particular. Most of his time is consumed in helping and understanding the Tribal and rural population of the region and writing scholarly articles and books on his vast area of interest.

Books written by the Author are –

1. Theory of Indian Cookery
2. Beauty and Irony of Silvassa Tourism
3. A Short Indian Food Story
4. Be Your Own Guide to Indian Cuisine
5. Cookery Fundamentals
6. History of Indian Food (2 Editions Printed)
7. The Great Indian Story Book for Children
8. Personal Budget: Easy Work Book
9. Online Classes Log Book
10. Dictionary Making Work Book for School Children
11. The Lazy Bed
12. Hindu Dharm (हिन्दू धर्म) (In Hindi Language)
13. Where is my coffee?
14. Your First Job is Never your Last (Volume 1)
15. You are Almost There (Quick Fix Resume and Interview Hacks)
16. Working for the Enemy? - A lesson in Career Management
17. Public Speaking for the Young
18. A Date With Coffee
19. How to be The Best Hotel Front Office Employee
20. Diploma in Food Production, The complete Syllabus
21. Diploma in F&B Service, The Complete Syllabus
22. Diploma in Front Office, The Complete Syllabus
23. The Time to Speak is Now
24. Munshi Premchand (Short Stories in English)
25. The Housekeeping Department, Text Book
26. Hitchhiker's Guide to Trekking in Uttarakhand

27. Uttarakhand, A divine Land for a Reason
28. Bachhon ke liye rochak kahaniyan (बच्चों के लिए रोचक कहानियाँ) (In Hindi Language)
29. Basic Communication Skills of English
30. The Basic Office Organisation Book for Start-ups
31. Hospitality HRM
32. Hospitality Marketing
33. Bakery Ingredients and Tools
34. Human Resource Management for Indian Professionals
35. The process of LAWFULLY operating a Hospitality business in India
36. Indian Classical Sweets: History, Tradition and Recipes
37. History of India's Himalayan Cuisine: Classical Cookery of Kashmir, Laddakh, Jammu, Himachal, Lahaul, Spiti, Garhwal, Kumaon.
38. Vindu: Andhra Cuisine (Part 1 of South Indian Trilogy)
39. Saappadu: Tamil Cuisine (Part 2 of South Indian Trilogy)
40. Sadya: Malayali Cuisine (Part 3 of South Indian Trilogy)
41. South Indian Cuisine - The Researcher's Guide Book
42. The Ramayana for Children and other short stories from Indian Mythology
43. Legends of the Tribal Shiva
44. Third Generation Children's Story Book
45. It's Elementary: The Top Nine Adventures from the memoirs of Dr John H Watson
46. UNITY IN DIVERSITY, The foundation of Indian Tourism
47. The Thar Express: Culinary History of Rajasthan and Gujarat
48. Basics of Computerized Accounting
49. Impact (Impact of Globalization on Indian Social Life)

Connect with me: anshumali.pandey@gmail.com
https://notionpress.com/author/337004

Please scan this QR code on you phone to know more about the latest and complete works of Dr Anshumali Pandey

9 798889 090526

Printed by Libri Plureos GmbH in Hamburg,
Germany